AF577263

The Penguin

This book has been reviewed
for accuracy by

Nathan E. Kraucunas
Acting Curator of Ornithology
Milwaukee Public Museum

Library of Congress Number: 78-21225

3 4 5 6 7 8 9 0 83

Printed in the United States of America.

Library of Congress Cataloging in Publication Data

Hogan, Paula Z
The penguin.

Cover title: The life cycle of the penguin.
SUMMARY: Explains in simple terms the life cycle of the penguin.
1. Penguins — Juvenile literature. [1. Penguins]
I. Strigenz, Geri K. II. Title. III. Title: The life cycle of the penguin.
QL696.S473H63 598.4'41 78-21225
ISBN 0-8172-1257-4 lib. bdg.

The PENGUIN

By Paula Z. Hogan
Illustrations by Geri K. Strigenz

RAINTREE CHILDRENS BOOKS
Milwaukee • Toronto • Melbourne • London

The rockhopper penguin is a fast swimmer. Every few minutes its head pops out of the sea so it can breathe.

Penguins cannot fly. Their wings are too small to lift them up. They use their wings like flippers for swimming.

Rockhoppers can climb high into the rocks. The penguins hop from rock to rock.

In spring, the rockhopper penguin jumps up on shore. It builds a nest of sticks and stones. The penguins try to take sticks and stones from each other. Rockhoppers are often fighting.

Soon the rockhopper hears his mate's call. They greet each other. She helps build the nest. After one month, she lays two eggs.

Rockhoppers almost always lose one egg. The parents take turns sitting on the nest. If danger is near, the feathers on the penguin's head will stick out.

Five weeks go by. The penguin chick hatches. The father keeps the chick safe. The mother feeds the chick.

In a month, the little penguin leaves the nest. It stays with many other chicks. When chicks are together, they are safe from other birds.

One chick walks off by itself. Down comes a big bird. Baby penguins are food for other animals.

In about four weeks, the little penguins begin to look like their parents. They grow smooth feathers. Now they can swim and catch fish.

The chicks are almost grown up. Now all rockhoppers go to sea. They swim and eat for over a month.

When the penguins come back, they lose their old feathers. They cannot swim without them. After they grow new feathers, the penguins go back to sea. This time they stay for about five months.

After long months at sea, the rockhopper penguins come back to the same island. They try to find the same mate. Together they will raise another chick.

There are many kinds of penguins. The emperor penguin is bigger than you are. The yellow-eyed penguin does not swim far from its home. The Galapagos penguin lives where the water is cold and the air is hot.

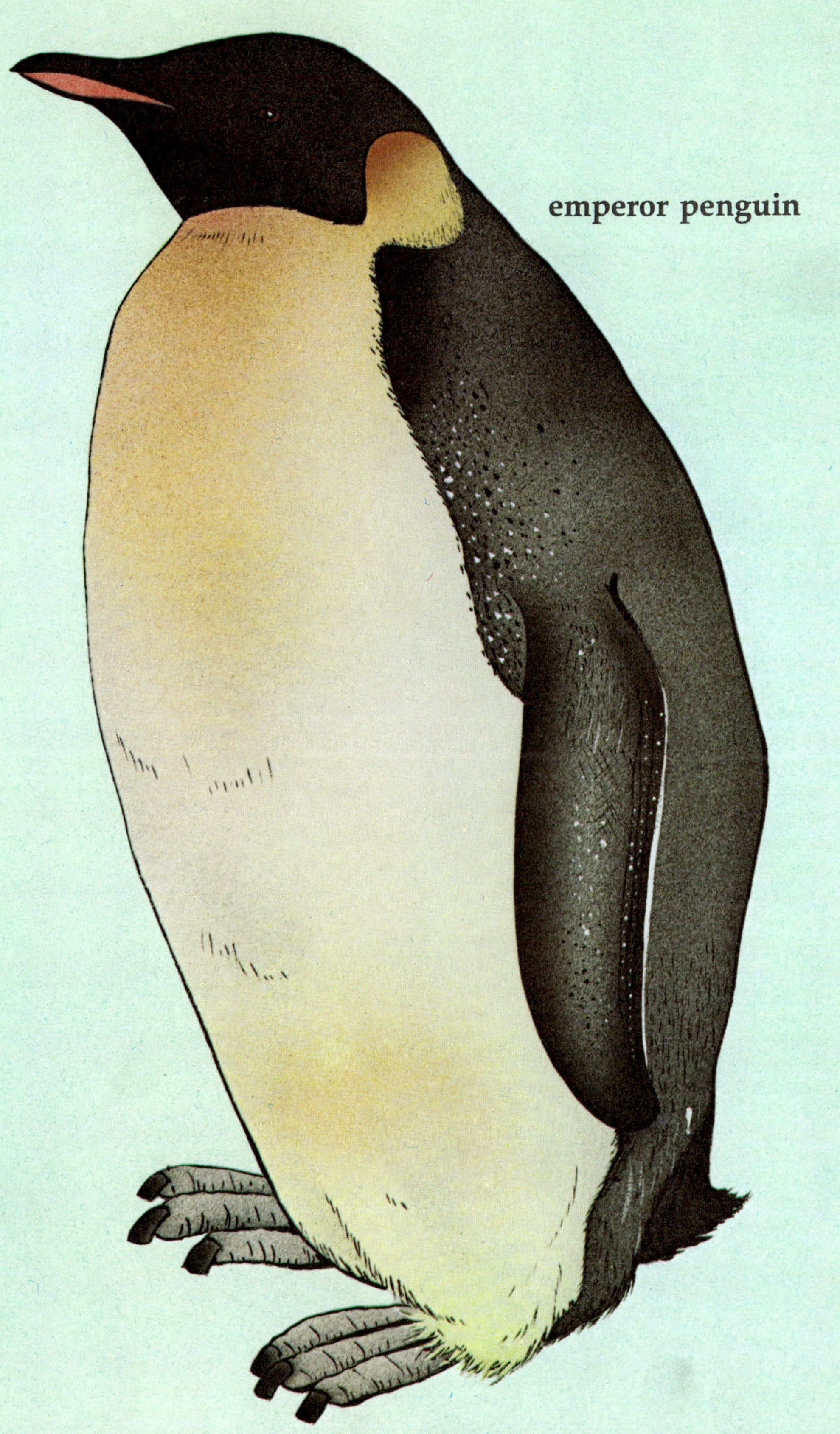
emperor penguin

GLOSSARY

These words are explained the way they are used in this book. Words of more than one syllable are in parentheses. The heavy type shows which syllable is stressed.

chick—a baby penguin

emperor penguin (**em**·per·or **pen**·guin)—the largest kind of penguin

flippers (**flip**·pers)—paddlelike wings used for swimming

Galapagos penguin (Ga·**la**·pa·gos **pen**·guin)—a kind of penguin that lives in warmer areas than most penguins

greet—to say hello

hatches (**hatch**·es)—egg opening to let a chick out

island (**is**·land)—land with water all around it

lose—to be not able to keep

mate—the male or female of a pair

raise—to have a baby and help it grow up

rockhopper (**rock**·hop·per)—a small kind of penguin with yellow feathers on its head

yellow-eyed penguin (**yel**·low – eyed **pen**·guin)—a kind of penguin with yellow eyes and a yellow area around its head